ENOUGH WATER?

A Guide to What We Have and How We Use It

ENOUGH

Introduction by **Steve Conrad**

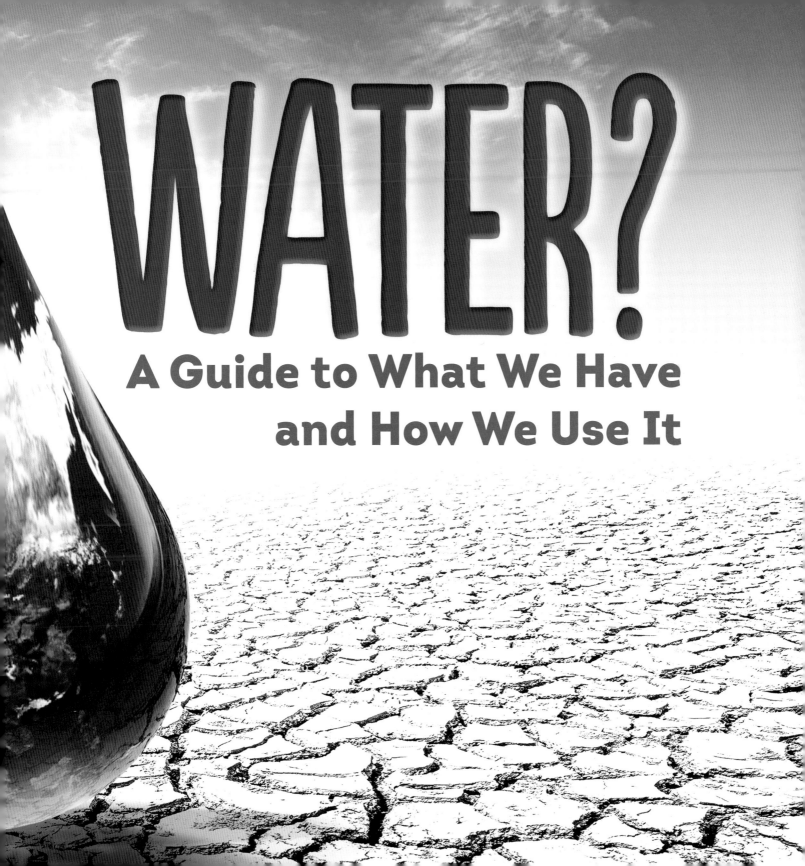

WATER?

A Guide to What We Have and How We Use It

A FIREFLY BOOK

Published by Firefly Books Ltd. 2016

First printing

Publisher Cataloging-in-Publication Data (U.S.)
Names: Editors of Firefly, authors. | Conrad, Steve, author introduction.
Title: Enough water? : A guide to what we have and how we use it / Editors of Firefly ; introduction by Steve Conrad.
Description: Richmond Hill, Ontario, Canada : Firefly Books, 2016. | Includes bibliography and index.
| Summary: "This guidebook focuses on our global health impact via "water footprints," how much freshwater is used to produce goods and services such as manufacturing, growing, harvesting, packaging, and shipping to market, which teaches young readers how to consume responsibly, and to think innovatively on sustainable freshwater alternatives" – Provided by publisher.
Identifiers: ISBN 978-1-77085-819-0 (hardcover) | 978-1-77085-818-3 (paperback)
Subjects: LCSH: Water-supply – Juvenile literature. | Water use – Juvenile literature. | Water conservation – Juvenile literature.
Classification: LCC TD348.E358 |DDC 333.91 – dc23

Library and Archives Canada Cataloguing in Publication
Enough water? : a guide to what we have and how we use it / editors of Firefly ; introduction by Steve Conrad.
Includes bibliographical references and index.
ISBN 978-1-77085-819-0 (hardback).–ISBN 978-1-77085-818-3 (paperback)
1. Water consumption–Juvenile literature. 2. Water use–Juvenile literature. 3. Water conservation–Juvenile literature. 4. Sustainable living–Juvenile literature. I. Firefly Books, author
TD348.C65 2016   j333.91'16   C2016-902314-1

Published in the United States by
Firefly Books (U.S.) Inc.
P.O. Box 1338, Ellicott Station
Buffalo, New York 14205

Published in Canada by
Firefly Books Ltd.
50 Staples Avenue, Unit 1
Richmond Hill, Ontario L4B 0A7

Cover and interior design: Hartley Millson

Printed in China

The publisher gratefully acknowledges the financial support for our publishing program by the Government of Canada through the Canada Book Fund as administered by the Department of Canadian Heritage.

While the publisher has made a serious attempt to obtain accurate information, the numbers represented in this book are for illustrative purposes only. Variances between sources and methodologies used for counting water footprints, areas, consumption and volume may not be reflected in the text or graphics. Subsequent editions of this book may contain updated values.

TABLE OF CONTENTS

INTRODUCTION

Every time you open a water faucet you are given a gift of clean, drinkable water. However, when was the last time you thought about where this water came from, or why it is that not everyone in the world has enough water? Well, in part, people struggle to find enough water because only a tiny amount of the world's water is drinkable and much of this water is trapped in ice or snow. People also struggle to find enough water because the choices we make in the food we eat and the products we buy affect the amount of water that is available to us.

In *Enough Water?* you will learn where your water comes from and you will learn where you use water at home. For instance, did you know that a family of four uses 45,000 liters (12,000 gallons) of water a year to wash clothes? That seems like a lot of water, and it is.

That amount of water would fill more than 300 bathtubs, and you would have to buy more than 110,000 bottles of water from a vending machine to equal that amount. If you stood those 110,000 bottles of water side by side you would have a line of bottles stretching for 9 kilometers (5.6 miles).

In *Enough Water?* you will also learn about how it takes water to grow the food we eat and make the products we buy. The more water it takes to grow or make something, the bigger the "water footprint" that item has. For example, it takes 7,600 liters (2,000 gallons) of water to make a pair of blue jeans, when you include all the water used in growing, processing, packaging and shipping the cotton used to produce them. And that glass of milk that many of us drink with our morning breakfast takes 200 liters (53 gallons) of water to make; that slice of toast takes 40 liters (10.5 gallons) of water. Every time you sit down for breakfast you are consuming all the "virtual water" it takes to make the food you eat. Sadly, our

bodies won't recognize the virtual water we consume, but we can reduce our water footprint by making different food choices and, more importantly, reducing food waste. Each time you throw food away, not only are you creating waste, you are also throwing away water. Throwing out a single banana wastes 160 liters (42 gallons) of water. This is the same as pouring 40 milk jugs of water down the drain. So make sure you don't end up throwing out your food choices, because you'll be wasting a lot more water than you may have imagined.

On every page, *Enough Water?* delivers an easy-to-understand illustration of water footprints across a variety of products and food items, from T-shirts to smartphones to apples and bananas. There is something in here for everyone who has ever wanted to know more about where water comes from and how water is used. After reading *Enough Water?* you will be better informed and inspired to look for ways to reduce your own individual water footprint.

ENOUGH WATER?

In school, we learn that people in places like Africa do not have enough water. California and other states suffer from drought. In your own house you may be asked to turn off the tap when brushing your teeth and take shorter showers. When you look at the globe in your classroom and you see that about two-thirds of the planet is covered in water, you wonder why there are water shortages. That's because only a very small amount of that water is usable or readily accessible for drinking, farming and making the things we use every day.

The images we see on the news can be confusing. On one hand we may witness instances where there is too much water, when places flood. On the other hand, we see farmers leaving their farms because

Baked, cracked earth where fertile land once existed (main), dried-up wetlands (top), dry lakebeds in California (middle) and sinking water levels in Lake Mead (bottom) indicate that our freshwater sources are becoming scarcer.

there is not enough water to grow anything. Both flooding and water scarcity are two sides of the same coin, and they can be blamed mostly on human activities. Filling in wetlands, which act like sponges to soak up excess rainwater, to create more farmland or sites for development is one key example. Another example is greenhouse gases released into the atmosphere when oil and gas are burned for transportation, generating electricity and home heating. The increase in greenhouse gases results in changing weather patterns. This causes more rain, rising sea levels and a warmer atmosphere.

As temperatures rise, giant frozen glaciers melt. Water is released from these glaciers into the world's oceans. One consequence is coastal flooding. As

Increasing levels of greenhouse gases cause extreme weather. Flooding around Donmaung Airport in Bangkok in 2011 may have been the result of changing climate, which brought excessive amounts of rain to the region during monsoon season (top).

A flooded roadway (middle) reveals the power of nature and the likely result of a rise in sea levels brought on by melting glaciers.

In drought-prone Australia, extreme weather events such as a tropical cyclone can result in too much of a good thing. An aerial view of the residential area of the suburb of Milton during the great Brisbane flood of 2011 reveals submerged homes (bottom).

the oceans rise and flood our shorelines, saltwater is absorbed by the ground and contaminates freshwater used for drinking and farming. In California, where farmers have depended on melting snow high up in the Sierra Nevada mountain range to water their crops, a warmer climate has eliminated the possibility of cold weather needed to make snow. Where melting snow once turned to water and trickled down streams and rivers to nourish California's farms, these farms are turning to dust. In other places, water for farms is pumped from underground sources. Farmland dries out when there is no more water in the ground for crops.

Water is the basis of all life on Earth and we should avoid wasting it. Consider that the next time you raise a refreshing glass of water to your lips.

IF THE WORLD'S WATER FILLED AN...

18-LITER (5-GALLON) WATER-COOLER BOTTLE

The available freshwater would be equivalent to

ONLY 3 TEASPOONS OF DRINKABLE WATER

97.5% of all the water on Earth is saltwater. The remaining 2.5% is freshwater. Almost all freshwater is locked up in polar icecaps, glaciers, snow and permafrost. If the world's water filled an 18-liter (5-gallon) water-cooler bottle, the available freshwater would contribute only 3 teaspoons.

WHAT IS A WATER FOOTPRINT?

A "water footprint" is the amount of freshwater used to grow food and make the things we use. Think of the impression your foot makes in the sand on a beach. The more footprints in the sand, the more water used. The water footprint required to grow a tomato is 50 liters (13 gallons) of water. It takes 910 liters (240 gallons) of water to make a smartphone, and 2,500 liters (660 gallons) to make a cotton T-shirt.

WHAT HAPPENS AT HOME!

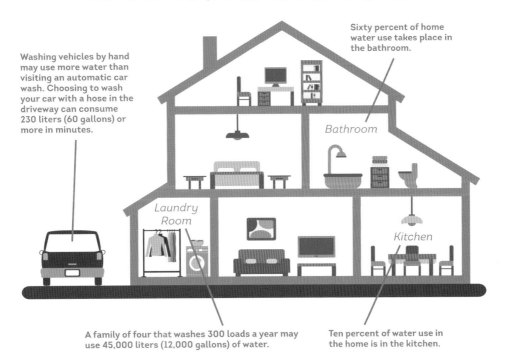

Washing vehicles by hand may use more water than visiting an automatic car wash. Choosing to wash your car with a hose in the driveway can consume 230 liters (60 gallons) or more in minutes.

Sixty percent of home water use takes place in the bathroom.

Bathroom

Laundry Room

Kitchen

A family of four that washes 300 loads a year may use 45,000 liters (12,000 gallons) of water.

Ten percent of water use in the home is in the kitchen.

WHERE DOES TAP WATER COME FROM?

Depending on where you live, water may come from a freshwater source such as a nearby lake, river or reservoir; from deep in the ground through a drilled well; or from a desalination plant that purifies ocean water and removes salt and minerals before it flows into your pipes. Water flows through large underground pipes (called water mains) below streets and sidewalks, and connects to your home's smaller water supply pipes. The water is pumped under pressure, so when you turn the tap, it gushes out.

WATER MAIN

Home

The water that comes out of your tap can come from different sources before it is piped underground to your home.

Wells

Well water is extracted from water that collects underground. Some wells need to be drilled very deep into the ground to reach the level where water Is present. Pumping too much water from the ground can deplete the natural water table, causing a well to "run dry."

Freshwater (lakes, streams, rivers)

Water taken from large bodies of water, rivers and streams is filtered and then pumped into the main water system, eventually reaching a home.

THE 10 BIGGEST AMERICAN CITIES RUNNING OUT OF WATER

RANKED BY POPULATION

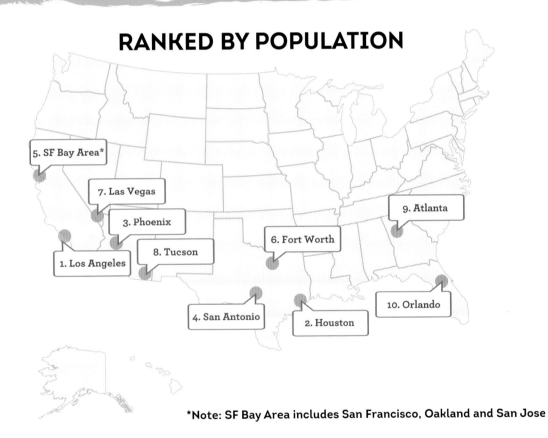

*Note: SF Bay Area includes San Francisco, Oakland and San Jose

Some of America's largest cities are in danger of running out of water. San Antonio and Orlando face immediate shortages. Los Angeles, Las Vegas and Atlanta have all faced severe water shortages in the past and are projected to do so again. Houston and Tucson have been identified as the cities with the highest risk of water shortage.

AVERAGE RESIDENTIAL WATER USE BY AMERICANS

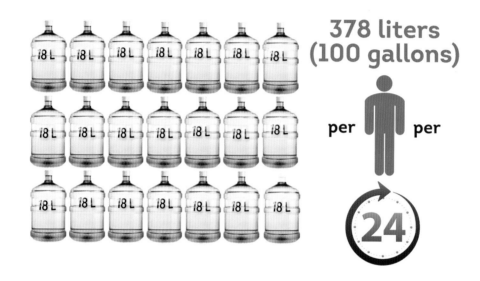

378 liters (100 gallons)

per **person** per **24** hours

Top 5 Highest Use in Liters (Gallons) per Day

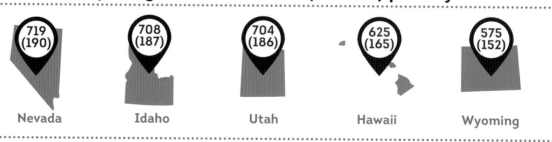

719 (190)	708 (187)	704 (186)	625 (165)	575 (152)
Nevada	Idaho	Utah	Hawaii	Wyoming

AVERAGE RESIDENTIAL WATER USE BY CANADIANS

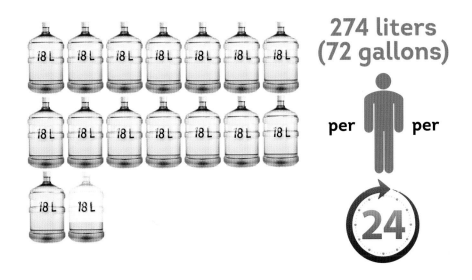

**274 liters
(72 gallons)**

per   per

24

Top 5 Highest Use in Liters (Gallons) per Day

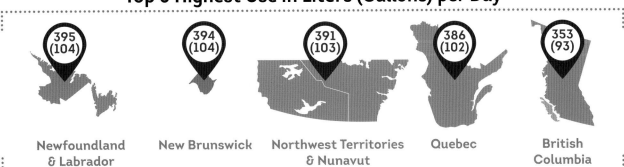

Newfoundland & Labrador	New Brunswick	Northwest Territories & Nunavut	Quebec	British Columbia
395 (104)	394 (104)	391 (103)	386 (102)	353 (93)

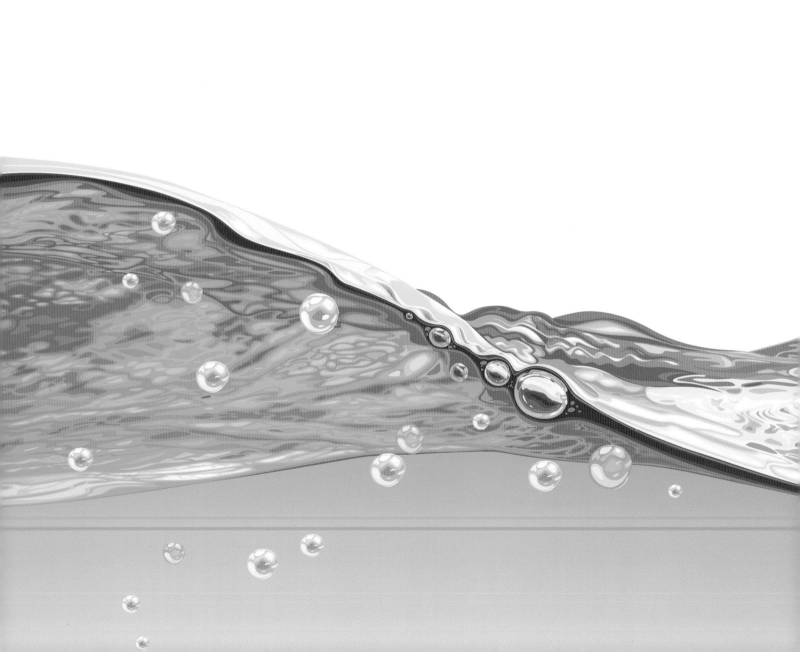

WATER BY THE NUMBERS

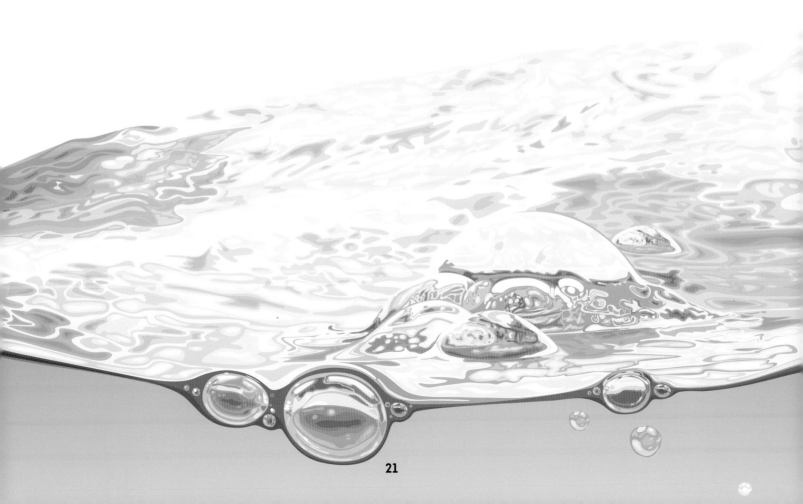

A 10-MINUTE SHOWER USES

160–190 LITERS (40–50 GALLONS) OF WATER

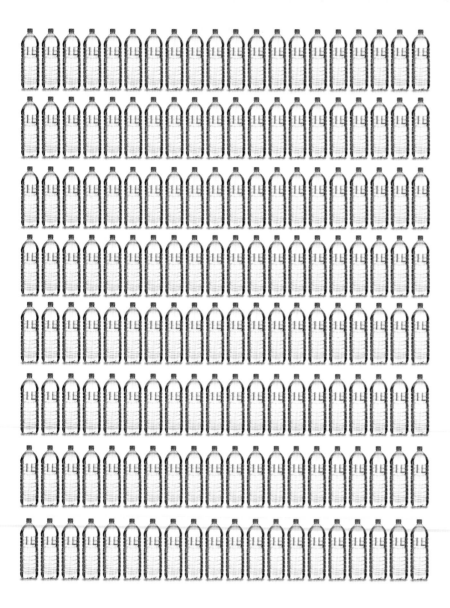

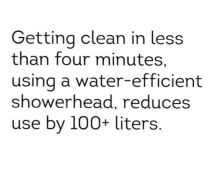

Getting clean in less than four minutes, using a water-efficient showerhead, reduces use by 100+ liters.

FLUSHING THE TOILET USES

APPROXIMATELY 18 LITERS (5 GALLONS) OF WATER

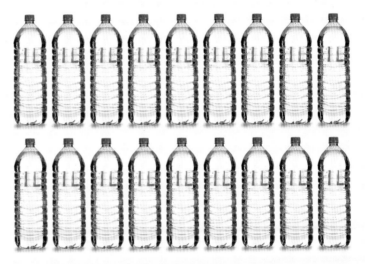

We go to the toilet about 5 times a day. Each flush uses about 3.75 liters (1 gallon). If you flush 5 times a day, that means you use about 18 liters (5 gallons) of water.

THE WATER FOOTPRINT OF 1 DISPOSIBLE DIAPER IS

545 LITERS (144 GALLONS) OF WATER

Disposable diapers require a whopping 545 liters (144 gallons) to make. A baby may use 5 diapers a day, which means 2,725 liters (720 gallons) of water is used.

TOOTHBRUSHING USES

6 LITERS (1.5 GALLONS) OF WATER A MINUTE

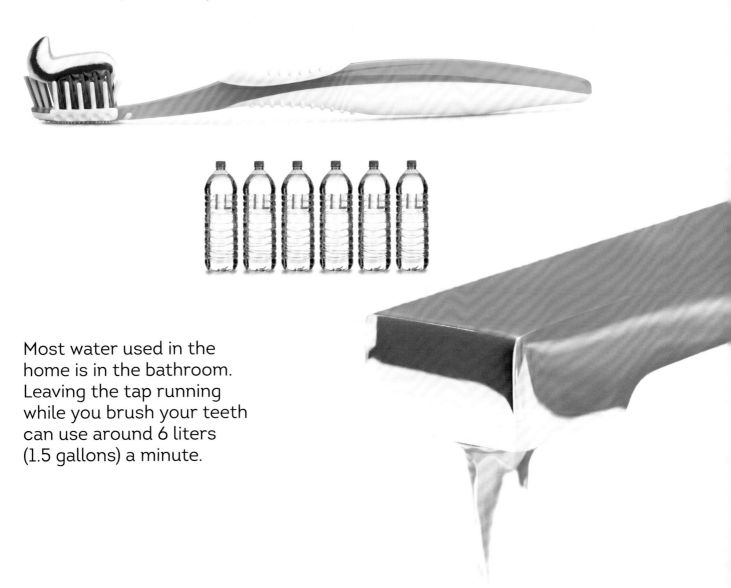

Most water used in the home is in the bathroom. Leaving the tap running while you brush your teeth can use around 6 liters (1.5 gallons) a minute.

1 LOAD OF LAUNDRY USES

MORE THAN 150 LITERS (40 GALLONS) OF WATER IN AN OLDER-MODEL WASHING MACHINE

An older washing machine may use more than twice as much water to get clothes clean than a newer model.

MORE THAN 76 LITERS (20 GALLONS) OF WATER IN A HIGH-EFFICIENCY WASHING MACHINE

Newer, high-efficiency machines use about 76 liters (20 gallons) to launder a load of clothes. A family of four that does 300 loads a year uses 22,700 liters (6,000 gallons) of water.

DISHWASHERS USE

36 LITERS (9.5 GALLONS) OF WATER PER LOAD

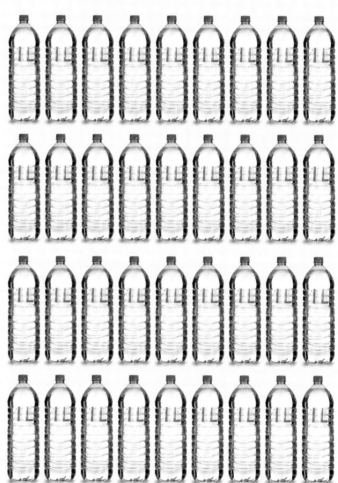

TO PRODUCE 1 PAIR OF JEANS REQUIRES

7,600 LITERS (2,000 GALLONS) OF WATER

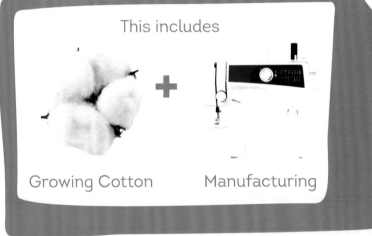

This includes

Growing Cotton + Manufacturing

It takes more than 7,600 liters (2,000 gallons) to make a typical pair of jeans. This does not include water used in laundering them over their lifetime, which would produce an even more staggering result.

TO PRODUCE 1 SMARTPHONE REQUIRES

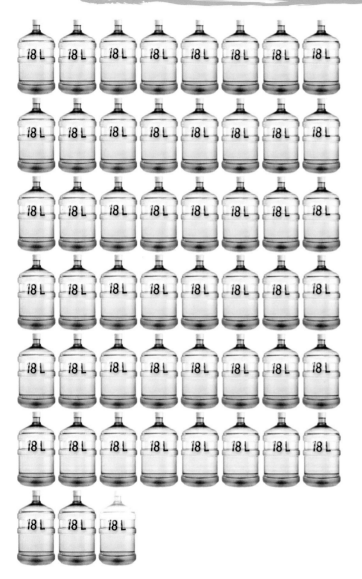

910 LITERS (240 GALLONS) OF WATER

Cellphones and smartphones use water throughout their production process, from creating the microchips to mining the metals used in the batteries to polishing the silica glass used in their touch screens. In total, each phone requires about 910 liters (240 gallons) of water to manufacture.

TO PRODUCE 1 INTEGRATED CIRCUIT BOARD FOR A HANDHELD GAME

REQUIRES 4,165 LITERS (1,100 GALLONS) OF WATER

To make microchips requires lots of water. Silicon semiconductors with integrated circuits must be scrubbed free of debris with the cleanest water possible.

TO PRODUCE 1 KILOGRAM (2 POUNDS) OF PAPER REQUIRES

3,000 LITERS
(793 GALLONS)
OF WATER

TO PRODUCE 1 COTTON SHIRT REQUIRES

Nearly 11,000 liters (2,900 gallons) of water is needed to produce 1 kilogram (2 pounds) of printed cotton textile. Thus a 250-gram (9-ounce) cotton shirt has a water footprint of 2,750 liters (725 gallons). Polyester has a nearly zero water footprint because manufacturing the polymer uses very little water.

2,750 LITERS (725 GALLONS) OF WATER

TO PRODUCE 1 POLYESTER SHIRT REQUIRES

350 LITERS (92.5 GALLONS) OF WATER

1 SLICE (30 GRAMS) OF BREAD

That dry slice of toast from the toaster in the morning is actually very wet, requiring some 40 liters (10 gallons) of water to grow and mill the wheat from which it is made, bake it, package it and deliver it to the store.

REQUIRES MORE THAN 40 LITERS (10 GALLONS) OF WATER

1 LOAF OF BREAD TAKES 520 LITERS (137 GALLONS) OF WATER

1 GLASS OF MILK REQUIRES

MORE THAN 200 LITERS (53 GALLONS) OF WATER TO PRODUCE

When you wash down those after-school cookies with a refreshing 250 ml (8-ounce) glass of milk, consider that you are actually consuming as much as 200 liters (53 gallons) of water, when you take into account the total amount of water required to feed the cow, package the milk, transport it and deliver it to your kitchen table.

TO GROW 1 APPLE

REQUIRES 125 LITERS (33 GALLONS) OF WATER

18 L 18 L 18 L 18 L 18 L 18 L 18 L

One 150-gram (5-ounce) apple costs 125 liters (33 gallons) of water. One 200-milliliter (7-ounce) glass of apple juice requires about 230 liters (60 gallons) of water.

1 ORANGE REQUIRES

80 LITERS (21 GALLONS) OF WATER

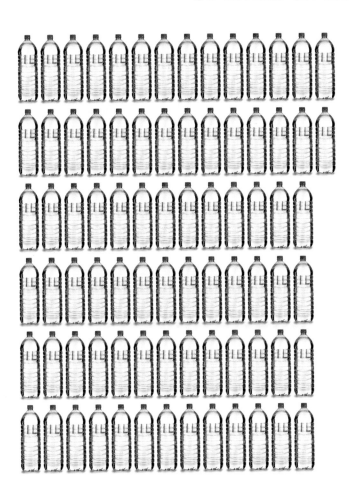

One 150-gram (5-ounce) orange requires 80 liters (21 gallons) of water to grow. A 200-milliliter (7-ounce) glass of orange juice requires about 200 liters (53 gallons) of water.

TO GROW 1 PINEAPPLE REQUIRES

130 LITERS (34 GALLONS) OF WATER

Pineapples require less water to grow than some other fruits. But as with other fruits, making juice out of the fruit requires an enormous amount of water. To make 4 liters (1 gallon) of pineapple juice requires about 1,360 liters (360 gallons) of water.

1 WATERMELON REQUIRES

At 92% water, a watermelon naturally requires a lot of water to grow—it needs constant watering or irrigation during the crop season. A 5-kilogram (11-pound) Green Giant or Crimson Sweet will soak up more than 1,000 liters (264 gallons) of water during its growth, harvesting and distribution.

1,000 LITERS (264 GALLONS) OF WATER

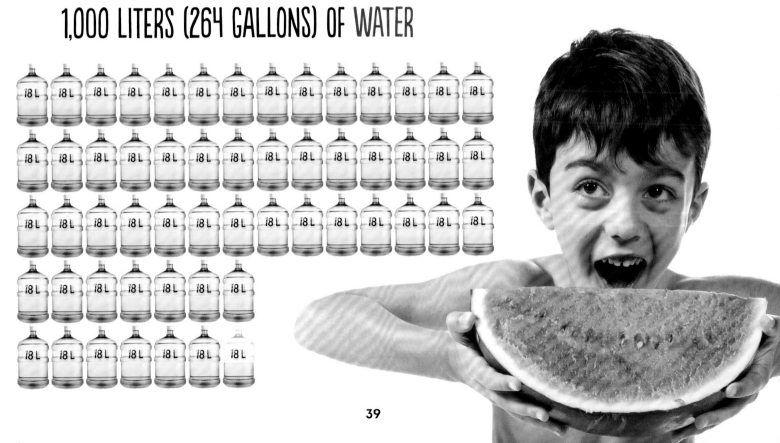

TO GROW A LEMON/LIME REQUIRES

Although they are small, lemons and limes require much more water than their size would suggest. Produce grown closer to home requires less energy and water to transport, but enjoying these sour fruits may mean importing virtual water from warmer, less water-rich regions, depending on where you live.

19 LITERS (5 GALLONS) OF WATER

TO PRODUCE 1 KILOGRAM OF BANANAS

REQUIRES 790 LITERS (209 GALLONS) OF WATER

The banana is one of the world's most popular fruits—Americans eat more bananas yearly than apples and oranges combined. To grow and process bananas takes about 790 liters (209 gallons) of water for every kilogram (2 pounds), or about 160 liters (42 gallons) per banana.

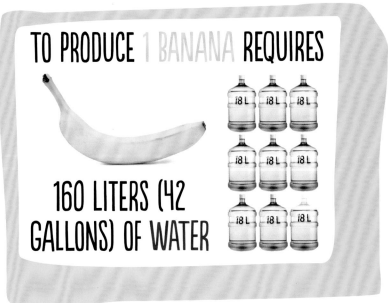

TO PRODUCE 1 BANANA REQUIRES

160 LITERS (42 GALLONS) OF WATER

TO PRODUCE 1 TOMATO REQUIRES

50 LITERS (13 GALLONS) OF WATER

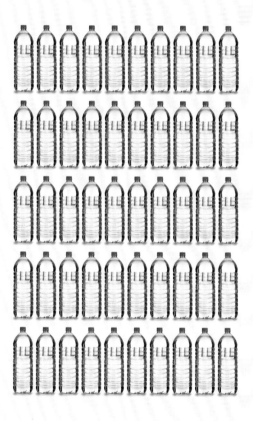

The tomato is one of the world's most important foods. Around 115 million tonnes (127 million tons) of the fruit are produced every year.

1 KILOGRAM (35 OUNCES) KETCHUP

REQUIRES 530 LITERS (140 GALLONS) OF WATER

Ketchup requires more than twice the amount of water than is needed to grow the tomatoes.

TO PRODUCE 1 CUP OF COFFEE

REQUIRES 140 LITERS (37 GALLONS) OF WATER

Making coffee is one of the largest uses of drinking water in North America. One cup (8 fluid ounces) of coffee requires 140 liters (37 gallons) of water.

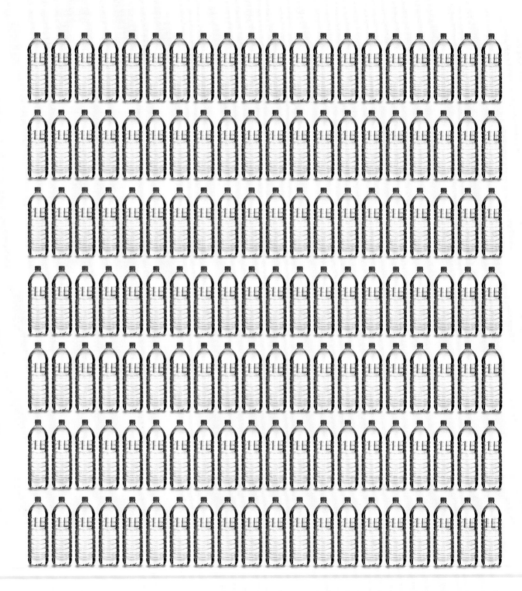

TO PRODUCE 1 CUP OF TEA

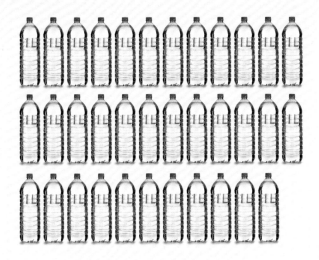

REQUIRES 35 LITERS (9 GALLONS) OF WATER

The virtual water content of tea consists mainly of rainwater. The dried black tea leaves needed for 1 cup (8 fluid ounces) of tea using a single teabag require around 35 liters (9 gallons) of water to grow, process and brew.

TO PRODUCE 1 KILOGRAM (2 POUNDS) OF MILLED RICE REQUIRES

2,500 LITERS (660 GALLONS) OF WATER

A staple food for 3 billion people, rice is also one of the largest water consumers in the world. On average, rice requires 2,500 liters (660 gallons) of water to yield only 1 kilogram (2 pounds) of milled rice.

TO PRODUCE 1 KILOGRAM (2 POUNDS) OF DRY PASTA REQUIRES

1,850 LITERS (490 GALLONS) OF WATER

A SINGLE SPAGHETTI NOODLE

REQUIRES 1.85 LITERS (0.5 GALLON) OF WATER

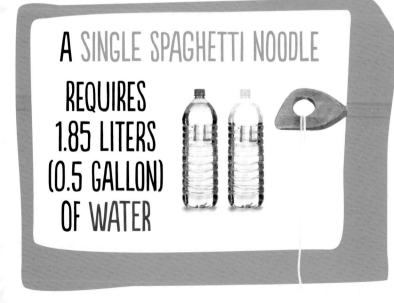

At its most basic, pasta is made from durum wheat semolina and water. The water footprint of pasta will vary depending on the sauce you serve with it. A simple tomato sauce includes the water footprint of tomatoes, and pasta primavera that of fresh vegetables.

47

TO PRODUCE 1 BOTTLE OF COLA

REQUIRES 175 LITERS (46 GALLONS) OF WATER

Cola is almost entirely water, so a half-liter (17-fluid-ounce) bottle effectively contains a half-liter of water. That's the direct water input. But cola is not just water in a bottle. When you include production of all the flavoring ingredients, the manufacturing and the supply chain, each bottle requires about 175 liters (46 gallons).

TO PRODUCE 1 CHOCOLATE BAR (200 GRAMS) REQUIRES

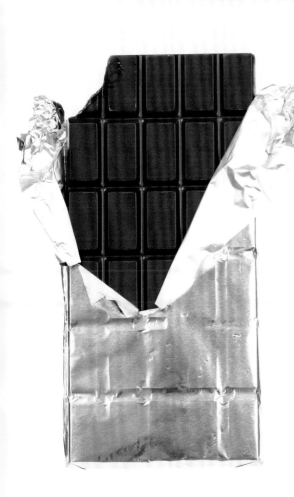

1,700 LITERS (450 GALLONS) OF WATER

Chocolate is made from ingredients with large water footprints: cocoa paste, cocoa butter and cane sugar. Cocoa beans are native to rainforests and require vast amounts of water to thrive.

TO PRODUCE 1 SMALL PIZZA MARGHERITA

REQUIRES 1,260 LITERS (333 GALLONS) OF WATER

The global average water footprint of one 725-gram (26-ounce) pizza margherita is 1,260 liters (333 gallons).

WATER BREAKDOWN PER INGREDIENT

Mozzarella Cheese	Wheat Flour	Tomato Purée
50%	44%	6%

TO PRODUCE 1 CHEESEBURGER

REQUIRES 2,400 LITERS (634 GALLONS) OF WATER

A typical 160-gram (6-ounce) cheeseburger requires 2,400 liters (634 gallons) of water to produce. Most of the water is needed for producing the beef. Including a slice of cheese and a bun adds about 100 liters (26 gallons) of water.

TO PRODUCE 1 LARGE EGG

REQUIRES 196 LITERS (52 GALLONS) OF WATER

On average worldwide, one 60-gram (2-ounce) egg requires 196 liters (52 gallons) of water to produce. Most of this is required for feeding the chickens.

TO PRODUCE 1 STICK OF BUTTER

REQUIRES 1,387 LITERS (366 GALLONS) OF WATER

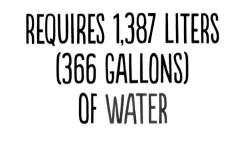

A 250-gram (9-ounce) stick of butter takes about 1,387 liters (366 gallons) of virtual water to produce.

TO PRODUCE 1 KILOGRAM (2 POUNDS) OF BEEF REQUIRES

15,400 LITERS (4,068 GALLONS) OF WATER

Animal products almost always have a larger water footprint than crops because of the massive amounts of feed needed to nourish livestock. Feed crops account for a whopping 99% of beef's water footprint.

That's almost 1.5 times the volume of a concrete mixer truck

TO PRODUCE 2 LAMB CHOPS

REQUIRES 10,400 LITERS
OF WATER PER KILOGRAM
(2,747 GALLONS PER 2 POUNDS)

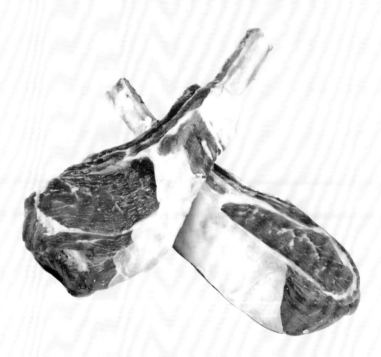

Compared to beef, which requires huge amounts of water to produce, lamb requires less water but still has a large footprint.

TO PRODUCE 2 PORK CHOPS

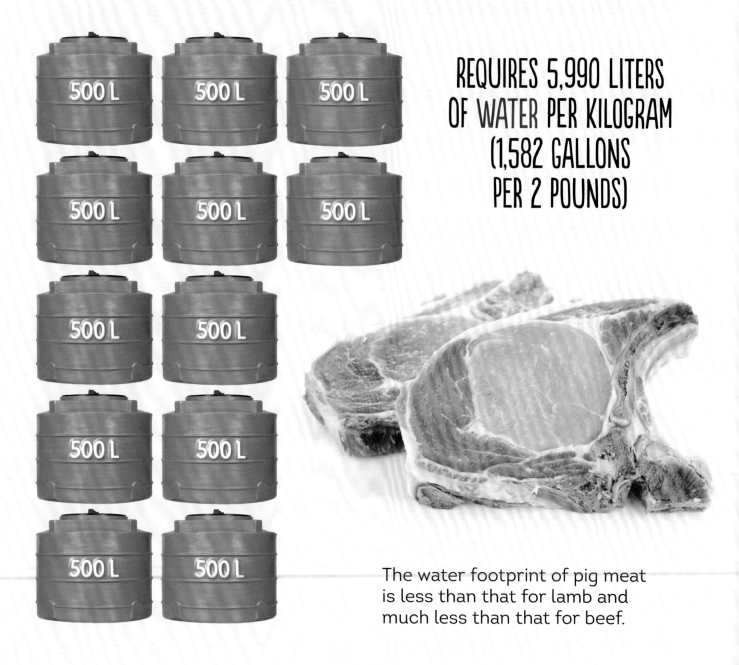

500 L · 500 L · 500 L
500 L · 500 L · 500 L
500 L · 500 L
500 L · 500 L
500 L · 500 L

REQUIRES 5,990 LITERS OF WATER PER KILOGRAM (1,582 GALLONS PER 2 POUNDS)

The water footprint of pig meat is less than that for lamb and much less than that for beef.

TO PRODUCE 6 CHICKEN LEGS

500 L 500 L
500 L 500 L
500 L 500 L
500 L 500 L
500 L

REQUIRES 4,300 LITERS OF WATER PER KILOGRAM (1,136 GALLONS PER 2 POUNDS)

When compared to other varieties of meat products, the water used for chicken meat is less than the footprints of meat from beef cattle, sheep, pigs and goats.

A MEAT-BASED DIET

CONSUMES THE EQUIVALENT OF 15 LARGE BATHTUBS OF WATER—DAILY

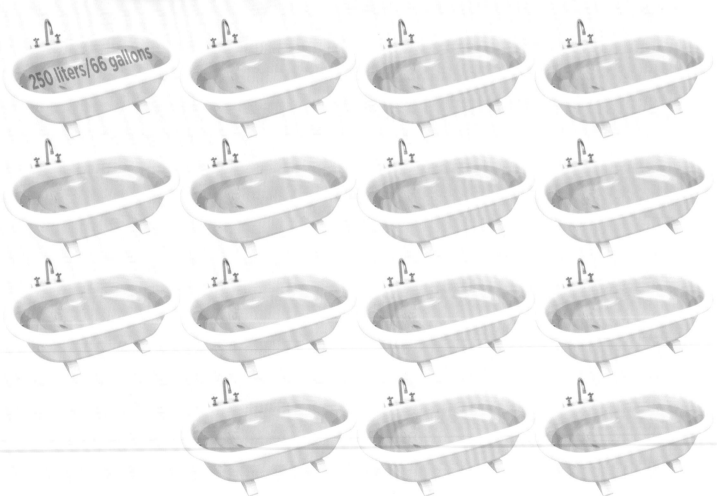

250 liters/66 gallons

A VEGETARIAN DIET

CONSUMES THE EQUIVALENT OF 8 BATHTUBS OF WATER—DAILY

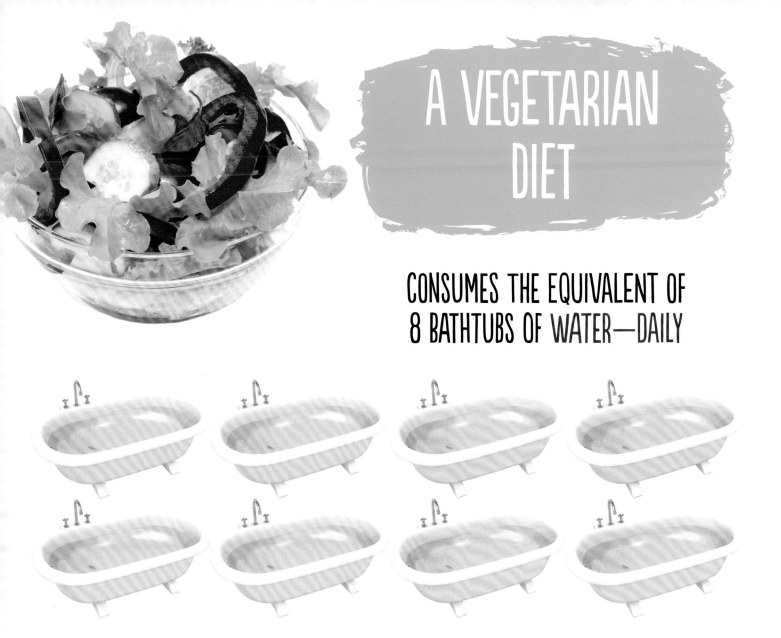

A meat-based diet of 3,400 calories per day uses between 3,600 and 5,000 liters (950–1,320 gallons) of water daily. The water used for a vegetarian diet is considerably smaller—2,300 to 2,700 liters (610–715 gallons) per day.

WATER-SAVING TIPS
(FOR CHILDREN AND ADULTS)

Everything we do, from eating and drinking to your parents' daily commutes, uses water (a lot goes into producing gas and energy). The clothes we wear require water to produce, and the products we buy also use water in their manufacture. Our daily water footprint includes more than the water we drink and use in our homes. Besides choosing less water-intensive products (for example, polyester versus cotton), we can take steps to limit the size of our water footprint in everyday activities such as lawn watering, clothes washing and flushing the toilet.

By knowing how dependent we are on water, not only for our health but for our modern lifestyle, we can change what we do. We can reduce wastage, change habits and make water-smart product purchases, all of which can save both water and money.

BATHROOM, KITCHEN AND LAUNDRY

- Take shorter showers and limit baths.
- Don't let the water run while brushing your teeth.
- Install aerators on faucets and use water-saving showerheads.
- Replace older toilets with newer, water-saving ones that use only 6 liters (1.6 gallons) per flush. The initial expense is worth it in the long run.
- Avoid flushing the toilet unnecessarily. Dispose of tissues, insects and other such waste in the trash rather than the toilet.
- Check for toilet leaks by adding food coloring to the tank. If the toilet is leaking, color will appear in the bowl within 30 minutes. (Flush as soon as the test is done, since the food coloring may stain.)
- Tell your parents to make sure that your home's pipes are leak-free. Many homes have hidden water leaks. Check your water meter and then read it after a two-hour period when no water is being used. If the reading is not exactly the same, there is a leak.
- Repair dripping faucets by replacing washers. One drop per second can waste 10,225 liters (2,700 gallons) per year, which will add to the cost of water and sewer utilities and/or strain your septic system.
- Use the minimum amount of water for a bath by filling the tub only one-third full. Stopper the tub before turning on the water.

61

BATHROOM, KITCHEN AND LAUNDRY

- Dishwashers should be fully loaded for optimum water conservation. There is usually no need to pre-rinse dishes.
- When washing dishes by hand, don't leave the water running for rinsing. If you have a double sink, fill one side with soapy water and one with rinse water. If you have a single basin, place the washed dishes in a rack and rinse them with a spray device or a pan full of hot water.
- Compost organic waste instead of using kitchen-sink garbage disposal units, which require lots of water to operate properly and put a strain on purification and septic systems.
- Don't let the faucet run while you clean vegetables. Rinse them in a stoppered sink or a pan of clean water.
- Keep a bottle or pitcher of drinking water in the fridge. Running tap water to cool it off for drinking is wasteful. Take refillable water bottles with you on outings.
- When washing clothes, avoid the permanent press cycle, which uses an additional 20 liters (5 gallons) for the extra rinse. For partial loads, adjust water levels to match the size of the load. Replace old laundry appliances. New Energy Star–rated washers use 35% to 50% less water and 50% less energy per load. If your household is in the market for a new clothes washer, consider buying a water-saving front-loading machine.

OUTDOORS

- Attach a rain barrel to downspouts to collect runoff from gutters (eaves-troughs). Use the collected water for the garden.
- Plant drought-resistant lawns, shrubs and plants. If you are planting a new lawn or reseeding an existing lawn, use drought-resistant grasses.
- Plant slopes with plants that will retain water and help reduce runoff. Group plants according to their watering needs.
- Apply a layer of mulch around trees and plants. Mulch slows evaporation of moisture while discouraging weed growth. Adding 5-10 centimeters (2-4 inches) of organic material such as compost or bark mulch will increase the soil's ability to retain moisture. Press down the mulch around the drip line of each plant to form a slight depression, which will prevent or minimize water runoff.
- Avoid overwatering plants and shrubs. This can actually diminish plant health and cause yellowing of the leaves.
- Many beautiful shrubs and plants can thrive with far less watering than other species. Replace herbaceous perennial borders with native plants, which use less water and are more resistant to local plant diseases. Consider applying the principles of xeriscaping for a low-maintenance, drought-resistant yard.
- Position your sprinklers so that the water lands on the lawn or garden, not on paved areas.
- Water your lawn only when it needs it. A good way to find out if your lawn needs watering is to step on the grass. If it springs back when you lift your foot, it doesn't need water. If it stays flat, the lawn is ready for watering. Letting the grass grow taller—to about 8-10 centimeters (3-4 inches)—will also promote water retention in the soil.
- Add organic matter to garden soil to help increase its absorption and water retention. Areas that are already planted can be top-dressed with compost or organic matter.

- Most lawns need only about 2.5 centimeters (1 inch) of water per week. During dry spells you can stop watering altogether: the lawn will turn brown and go dormant. Once cooler weather arrives, the morning dew and rainfall will bring the grass back to its usual vigor. This may result in a brown summer lawn but it saves a lot of water.
- Deep-soak your lawn. When watering, do it long enough for the moisture to soak down to the roots, where it will do the most good. A light sprinkling can evaporate quickly and tends to encourage shallow root systems. Put an empty tuna can on your lawn—when it's full, you've watered about the right length of time.
- Early or late watering reduces water loss due to evaporation. Early morning is generally better than dusk, since it helps prevent the growth of fungus, and watering early in the day is also the best defense against slugs and other garden pests. Try not to water when it's windy; wind can blow the water off target and speed evaporation.
- Use efficient watering systems for shrubs, flowerbeds and lawns. You can greatly reduce the amount of water used with soaker hoses or a simple drip irrigation system.
- Use a commercial drive-through car wash. Most car washes use recycled water for cleaning.
- If washing the car by hand, don't run the hose while washing. Clean the car first, using a pail of soapy water. Use the hose only for rinsing—this simple practice can save as much as 570 liters (150 gallons). Use a spray nozzle when rinsing for more efficient use of water.
- Sweep driveways and sidewalks clean instead of hosing them down.
- Check for leaks in outdoor pipes, hoses, faucets and couplings. Leaks outside the house may not seem so bad, since they're not as visible, but they can be just as wasteful as leaks indoors. Check frequently to keep them drip-free. Use washers at spigots and hose connections to eliminate leaks.

LIFESTYLE

- Drive less. In Alberta's oil sands, a barrel of oil takes about 2.5 barrels of water to produce, and most of the water used ends up in toxic tailings ponds because it's too polluted to return to the river. By driving less, you can become part of the solution to protect rivers such as the Athabasca.
- Create awareness of the need for water conservation among your children. Avoid purchasing recreational toys that require a constant stream of water.
- Be aware of and follow all water conservation and water shortage rules and restrictions that may be in effect in your area.
- Encourage your employer to promote water conservation in the workplace. Suggest that water conservation be made part of employee orientation and training.
- Encourage your school system and local government to help develop and promote a water conservation ethic among both children and adults.
- Support projects that will lead to increased use of reclaimed wastewater for irrigation and other uses.
- Report all significant water loss (broken pipes, open hydrants, errant sprinklers, abandoned free-flowing wells, etc.) to property owners, local authorities or public works departments.
- Support efforts and programs to create concern for water conservation among tourists and visitors to your area. Make sure visitors understand the need for and benefits of water conservation.
- Conserve water because it is the right thing to do. Don't waste water just because someone else is footing the bill, such as when you are showering at a health club or community center.

- Purchase secondhand clothing. The average water requirement to produce 1 kilogram (2 pounds) of cotton is 11,000 liters (2,900 gallons). This translates to a whopping 2,900 liters (766 gallons) to produce a plain cotton shirt! You can achieve big reductions in your water footprint by buying clothes secondhand or by wearing polyester, which requires much less water to produce.
- Patronize businesses that practice and promote water conservation.

- Encourage your friends and neighbors to be part of a water-conscious community. Promote water conservation in community newsletters, on bulletin boards and by example.
- Try to do one thing every day that will result in saving water. Don't worry if the savings are minimal. Every drop counts, and every person can make a difference. So tell your friends, neighbors and co-workers, "Turn it off and keep it off."

SELECTED BIBLIOGRAPHY

Aldaya, M. M., and A. Y. Hoekstra. *The Water Needed to Have Italians Eat Pasta and Pizza.* Value of Water Research Report Series no. 36. Delft: UNESCO-IHE Institute for Water Education, 2009. http://waterfootprint.org/media/downloads/Report36-WaterFootprint-Pasta-Pizza.pdf.

Appropedia. "LCA: Cloth vs. Disposable Diapers Introduction." November 17, 2011. http://www.appropedia.org/cloth_versus_disposable_diapers.

Bras, B., F. Tejada, J. Yen, J. Zullo and T. Guldberg. *Quantifying the Life Cycle Water Consumption of a Passenger Vehicle.* SAE International. April 16, 2012. http://www.manufacturing.gatech.edu/sites/default/files/uploads/pdf/2012-01-0646.pdf.

Brazzale. "Gran Moravia Is the First Cheese in the World to Set Its Water Footprint." September 2012. http://www.brazzale.com/gran-moravia-is-the-first-cheese-in-the-world-to-set-its-water-footprint/?lang=en.

Chapagain, A. K., and A. Y. Hoekstra. "The Water Footprint of Coffee and Tea Consumption in the Netherlands." *Ecological Economics* 64 (2007): 109–18. http://waterfootprint.org/media/downloads/ChapagainHoekstra2007waterforcoffeetea.pdf.

Chapagain, A. K., and A. Y. Hoekstra. *Water Footprints of Nations.* Value of Water Research Report Series no. 16. Delft: UNESCO-IHE Institute for Water Education, 2004. http://waterfootprint.org/media/downloads/Report16Vol1.pdf.

Chapagain, A. K., and A. Y. Hoekstra. *The Water Needed to Have the Dutch Drink Tea.* Value of Water Research Report Series no. 15. Delft: UNESCO-IHE Institute for Water Education, 2003. http://waterfootprint.org/media/downloads/Report15.pdf.

Chapagain, A. K., and S. Orr. *UK Water Footprint: The Impact of the UK's Food and Fibre Consumption on Global Water Resources.* Vol. 1. Surrey: World Wildlife Federation, 2008. http://assets.wwf.org.uk/downloads/water_footprint_uk.pdf.

Consumer Reports. "Shower or Bath: Which Uses More Water?" August 22, 2008. http://www.consumerreports.org/cro/news/2008/08/shower-or-bath-which-uses-more-water/index.htm.

De Beers. *Living Up to Diamonds: Report to Society 2010.* https://www.yumpu.com/en/document/view/29314454/de-beers-2010-report-to-society-anglo-american.

FAO (UN Food and Agriculture Organization) Water Development and Management Unit. "Crop Water Information: Tomato." http://www.fao.org/nr/water/cropinfo_tomato.html.

The Green Mama. "Analyzing Environmental Life-Cycle Costs of Diapers." http://oldsite.thegreenmama.com/analyzing-environmental-life-cycle-costs-diapers.

Hoekstra, A. Y. "The Hidden Water Resource Use Behind Meat and Dairy." *Animal Frontiers* 2, no. 2 (2012). http://waterfootprint.org/media/downloads/Hoekstra-2012-Water-Meat-Dairy.pdf.

Hoekstra, A. Y., and A. K. Chapagain. *Globalization of Water: Sharing the Planet's Freshwater Resources.* Oxford: Blackwell, 2008.

Hoekstra, A. Y., and A. K. Chapagain. "Water Footprints of Nations: Water Use by People as a Function of Their Consumption Pattern." *Water Resources Management* 21, no. 1 (January 2007): 35–48. http://waterfootprint.org/media/downloads/Hoekstra_and_Chapagain_2006.pdf.

Hoekstra, A. Y., and M. M. Mekonnen. "The Green, Blue and Grey Water Footprint of Crops and Derived Crop Products." *Hydrology and Earth System Sciences* 15 (2011): 1577–1600. http://doc.utwente.nl/77177/1/Mekonnen11green.pdf.

Hoekstra, A. Y., and M. M. Mekonnen. *National Water Footprint Accounts: The Green, Blue and Grey Water Footprint of Production and Consumption.* Value of Water Research Report Series no. 50. Delft: UNESCO-IHE Institute for Water Education, 2011. http://waterfootprint.org/media/downloads/Report50-NationalWaterFootprints-Vol1.pdf.

Kostigan, T. M. *The Green Blue Book.* Emmaus, PA: Rodale, 2010

Mekonnen, M. M., and A. Y. Hoekstra. *The Green, Blue and Grey Water Footprint of Farm Animals and Animal Products.* Value of Water Research Report Series no. 48. Delft: UNESCO-IHE Institute for Water Education, 2010. http://waterfootprint.org/media/downloads/Report-48-WaterFootprint-AnimalProducts-Vol1.pdf.

Natural Resources Canada. *2003 Survey of Household Energy Use (SHEU): Detailed Statistical Report.* Ottawa: Government of Canada, 2006. http://oee.nrcan.gc.ca/publications/statistics/sheu03/pdf/sheu03.pdf.

Oki, T. "Issues on Water Footprint and Beyond." Workshop presented at Global Environmental Centre Foundation, Tokyo, Japan, June 3, 2010. http://gec.jp/gec/en/Activities/ietc/fy2010/wf/wf_os-3e.pdf.

Ruini, L., M. Marino, S. Pignatelli, F. Laio and L. Ridolfi. "Water Footprint of a Large-Sized Food Company: The Case of Barilla Pasta Production." *Water Resources and Industry* 1–2 (March–June 2013): 7–24. http://www.sciencedirect.com/science/article/pii/S2212371713000061.

Soil & More International. *Water Footprint Assessment: Bananas and Pineapples, Dole Food Company.* May 2011. http://dolecrs.com/uploads/2012/06/Soil%20&%20More%20Water%20Footprint%20Assessment.pdf.

United States Environmental Protection Agency (EPA). "Indoor Water Use in the United States." WaterSense. http://www.epa.gov/watersense/pubs/indoor.html.

United States Geological Service. "Water Properties and Measurements." http://ga.water.usgs.gov/edu/waterproperties.html.

Waterwise. "Showers vs. Baths: Facts, Figures and Misconceptions." November 24, 2011. http://www.waterwise.org.uk/news.php/11/showers-vs.-baths-facts-figures-and-misconceptions.

GLOSSARY

Blue water footprint
The volume of surface and groundwater used during production, such as in growing fruits, vegetables and grains, as well as consumer products.

Climate change
A long-term change in weather patterns over periods of time that range from decades to millions of years.

Desalination
A process that removes the salt and other minerals from water in order to obtain freshwater suitable for consumption and irrigation.

Drought
A prolonged period of abnormally low rainfall or a shortage of water.

Glacier
A slow-moving mass or river of ice formed by the accumulation and compaction of snow on mountains or near the poles.

Gray water footprint
The amount of water required to restore water purity.

Green water footprint
The volume of rainwater used in production of fruits and vegetables.

Hurricane
A storm with a violent wind, in particular a tropical cyclone in the Caribbean.

Typhoon
A mature tropical cyclone that develops in the western part of the North Pacific Ocean.

Virtual water
Water experts Drs. A.Y. Hoekstra and A.K. Chapagain define the **virtual water** content of a product (a commodity, good or service) as "the volume of freshwater used to produce the product, measured at the place where the product was actually produced."

Water footprint
Total volume of freshwater used to produce the goods and services consumed by an individual or community or produced by a business. Water use is measured in water volume consumed (evaporated) and/or polluted per unit of time.

Wetland
Land consisting of marshes or swamps; land saturated by moisture and water.

CREDITS

All photos and illustrations courtesy of Shutterstock, copyright © its respective photographers and illustrators:

p.2-3 sakepaint;
p.8 Galyna Andrushko;
p.9 (top) Jeffrey B. Banke;
p.9 (middle) Radoslaw Lecyk;
p.9 (bottom) Tupungato;
p.10 (top) KAMONRAT / Shutterstock.com;
p.10 (middle) Dave Weaver;
p.10 (bottom) Brisbane;
p.11 Juancat;
p.12 (spoon) Alexi Bradich;
p.12 (left, throughout) Tarasyuk Igor;
p.13 (house) Elvetica;
p.14 Shayneppl;
p.15 (top) composite dashadima;
p.15 (middle) Denis Dryashkin;
p.15 (bottom) Artush;
p.16 Sean Pavone;
p.20-21 block23;
p.22 Eduard Stelmakh;
p.23 Mindscape studio;
p.24 (top) Dmitry Lobanov;
p.24 (bottom) Myotis;
p.25 (top) bergamont;
p.25 (middle, throughout) monticello;
p.25 (bottom) photopixel;

p.26 (right) NA;
p.27 (right) Ljupco Smokovski;
p.28 (left) ppart;
p.29 (left, throughout) Deamles for Sale;
p.29 (middle, left) mexrix;
p.29 (middle, right) Africa Studio;
p.29 (bottom) 5;
p.30 (right) Nik Merkulov;
p.31 (right) Dabarti CGI;
p.32 (bottom) Laborant;
p.33 (bottom, left) Maryna Kulchytska;
p.33 (bottom, right) exopixel;
p.34 (left) Dan Kosmayer;
p.34 (middle, left) johnfoto18;
p.34 (middle, right) Seregam;
P.35 (right) ILYA AKINSHIN;
p.36 (bottom) Dionisvera;
p37 (right) NinaM;
p.38 (right) indigolotos;
p.39 (top) S-F;
p.39 (bottom, right) Luis Molinero;
p.40 (top) zcw;
p.40 (bottom) rockstar_images;
p.41 (top, right) Peter Zijlstra;
p.41 (bottom, right) photolinc;
p.42. (right) Abramova Elena;
p.43 (right) g215;
p.43. (bottom) JPC-PROD;
p.44 (left) Africa Studio;
p.45 (right) Epitavi;

p.46 (bottom) liza54500;
p.47 (bottom, left) Thomas Bethge;
p.47 (bottom, right) Timmary;
p.48. (right) maradon 333;
p. 49 (left) prapass;
p.50 (left) Oxana Denezhkina;
p.50 (bottom, left) Dan Kosmayer;
p.50 (bottom, middle) kiboka;
p.50 (bottom, right) Louella938;
p.51 (bottom) BravissimoS;
p.52 (right) tankist276;
p.53 (left) Robyn Mackenzie;
p.54 (top) Dulce Rubia;
p.54 (bottom) StockPhotosArt;
p.55 (right) Chiyacat;
p.56 (right) margouillat photo;
p.57 (right) Dulce Rubia;
p.58 (top) Joe Gough;
pp.58-59 (middle) higyou;
p.59 (top) Meelena;
p.60 Porfang;
p.61 Evgeny Atamanenko;
p.63 India Picture;
p.67 Smith1972

INDEX